Who Was
Fidel Castro?

by Sarah Fabiny

illustrated by Ted Hammond

Penguin Workshop
An Imprint of Penguin Random House

To the revolutionary Who HQ team—SF

To my mom—TH

PENGUIN WORKSHOP
Penguin Young Readers Group
An Imprint of Penguin Random House LLC

Library of Congress Cataloging-in-Publication Data is available.

ISBN 9780451533333 (paperback)   10 9 8 7 6 5 4 3 2 1
ISBN 9780451533357 (library binding)   10 9 8 7 6 5 4 3 2 1

Contents

Who Was Fidel Castro?

"Fidel! Fidel! Fidel!" Hundreds of thousands of people gathered in the city of Havana, the capital of Cuba, were shouting for Fidel Castro. It was the evening of January 8, 1959. A week earlier, Fidel and his forces had overthrown President Batista and the government of Cuba. The crowds in Havana were waiting for their new leader to speak about his plans for the country.

Cubans were ready for the freedom and changes that Fidel had promised them. The Cuban people were ready for a new leader.

Spotlights shone on the stage where Fidel was to speak. Fidel finally stepped up to the microphone. He had a big, bushy beard and was dressed in

an army cap and olive-green army fatigues. The crowds cheered even louder when they saw Fidel.

Fidel spoke for two hours. He told everyone listening in Havana, across Cuba, and around the world that he was the new leader of the country. He would bring change to his beloved homeland.

As Fidel ended his speech, several white doves were released. One of the doves landed on Fidel's shoulder. The crowd went silent. White doves were seen as a sign of peace. Many believed it was a sign from God. They believed that Fidel, who was only thirty-two years old at the time, had been specially chosen to lead Cuba.

CHAPTER 1
A Privileged Childhood

Fidel Castro was born on August 13, 1926. His father was named Angel. He was the owner of a sugar cane plantation. (A plantation is a very large farm that usually grows only one crop.) He had immigrated to Cuba from Spain in 1905. Fidel's mother, Lina, was a housekeeper at the

plantation. Fidel was Angel and Lina's third child. After Fidel was born, the couple had four more children. Angel and Lina did not get married until Fidel was a teenager.

The sugar cane plantation where Fidel grew up was called Las Manacas. It was near the town of Biran. Biran is at the eastern end of Cuba. At the time, this area was among the poorest in Cuba. Most people lived in simple shacks without running water or electricity. They worked on small farms and plantations for hardly any money.

Fidel's father had started out like this. But he was determined to make a better life for himself. Angel taught himself to read and write. He worked hard and saved money so that he could buy his own property. Angel was proud to be able to give his own family the things he did not have as a child.

The plantation grew to over twenty-five thousand acres. Three hundred families lived and worked on the property. Although Fidel was the owner's son, he played with the children of the laborers who worked on the plantation. And workers often ate meals with Fidel and his family.

The History of Cuba

Today the island nation of Cuba has a population of about eleven million people. Native tribes called the Taino, Ciboney, and Guanahatabey lived in Cuba for thousands of years. They lived in small villages and hunted, fished, and grew crops such as sweet potatoes, corn, cotton, and tobacco. But this changed in 1492, when Christopher Columbus landed in Cuba. He claimed the island now belonged to Spain. The Spanish ruled Cuba for hundreds of years. Then, in 1895, Cubans fought a war against Spain and won independence in 1898. But the men who ruled Cuba after this were corrupt. They took bribes and cheated at elections. The last of these rulers was Fulgencio Batista. Fidel Castro overthrew him in 1959.

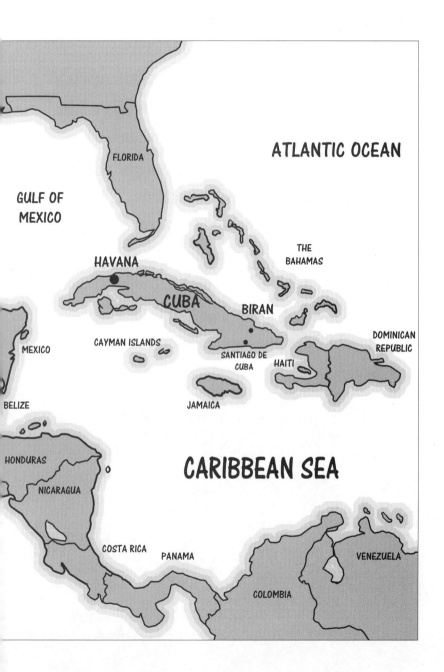

Fidel saw that his life was very different from the lives of the workers. The Castro children never worried about having enough to eat. They dressed in fine clothes and went to private schools. They rode horses, swam in the river, hunted, fished, and climbed in the nearby mountains.

Fidel spent a lot of time with his older brother Ramon and his younger brother Raul. The brothers were very close, especially Fidel and Raul. Raul looked up to Fidel, and Fidel always looked out for his younger brother.

From a very young age, Fidel had a stubborn streak and a strong temper. Although a bright boy, he had a hard time sitting still at school. Fidel argued with his teachers and fought with other students. He was always determined to get his own way.

When Fidel was about seven years old, his parents sent him to La Salle, a private Catholic boarding school. Ramon and Raul were also sent there. Their parents hoped that the boarding school would help their sons, especially Fidel, behave and be better students. But that did not happen. Fidel and his brothers did very little work and did not get good grades.

At the end of Fidel's fourth-grade year, Angel brought his sons home. He refused to send them back to school. Although Fidel didn't like school, he didn't want to be stuck at home. In fact, he threatened to burn down the family house! So Fidel's father gave in. But he decided to send Fidel to an even stricter school.

In 1940, Fidel moved to Dolores Academy. Raul joined his older brothers at the school when he was old enough to attend. The school's many

Fidel, Raul, and Ramon at Dolores Academy

rules had a good effect on Fidel. He studied more and his grades improved. Fidel also discovered he was good at sports. He made it onto the boxing, soccer, and baseball teams.

When he was sixteen, Fidel convinced his parents to let him go to the Jesuit preparatory school of Belen in Havana. It was the most exclusive high school in the country. In time, Raul joined his older brother there.

Fidel came from a rich family. Still, other boys saw Fidel as an outsider. Most of the students came from Havana. They were rich city boys and made fun of Fidel for being from the countryside. They called him a peasant behind his back.

A Letter to the President

On November 6, 1940, Fidel wrote a letter to the US president Franklin D. Roosevelt. In the letter he told the president that he listened to him on the radio. Fidel said he was happy that Roosevelt had won a third term in office. Fidel asked the president to send him a ten-dollar bill since he had never seen one. Fidel also said he would show the president the largest iron mines in Cuba. Fidel thought the United States might want the iron for shipbuilding. Fidel's letter received a reply from the White House. But it did not include a ten-dollar bill. For the rest of his life, Fidel spoke of his respect for Roosevelt, who helped the poor in the United States during the Great Depression. Today Fidel's letter is kept at the National Archives in Washington, DC.

Fidel decided that rather than fighting, he would turn his energy to his studies. Soon his hard work impressed his teachers—and the other students, too. Fidel graduated in the top ten of his class. His yearbook read "Fidel always distinguished himself in all subjects. . . . He was . . . a true athlete, always defending the banner of the school with pride and valor. He has won the admiration and affection of all . . . We do not doubt that

FIDEL CASTRO RUZ

Fidel has what it takes and will make something of his life."

CHAPTER 2
Student Days

During high school, Fidel had dreamed about playing baseball for a team in the United States. But when he graduated, he decided to study law. He realized that his strong will would make him a good lawyer. He enrolled in the University of Havana in 1945.

The university was a place to study and learn. But it was also a dangerous place. Cuba's political parties had student groups at the university. The political parties had different ideas about how to change the government, and so did the student groups. Discussions between the groups often turned into violent arguments that were settled with guns or knives.

Fidel took an interest in these groups. But he decided not to join any of them. Because Fidel did not belong to any one group, he was able to speak at the rallies of all the groups. (A rally is a large gathering of people to create enthusiasm for an idea or a cause.)

Fidel was not nervous about speaking in front of crowds. He discovered that he liked public speaking and was good at it. Fidel started thinking that a career in politics might be right for him. He started wearing a suit and tie on campus so other students would take notice of him.

The more Fidel's interest in politics grew, the more he came to see what was wrong in Cuba. He felt that the needs of poor people were being ignored. The leaders only cared about themselves and their power. He wanted to get rid of the corrupt government.

Fidel started speaking directly against the president of Cuba, Ramon Grau San Martin. Now the press and the government started to notice Fidel. But Fidel was not afraid. It was more important to him to speak up for his beliefs.

Ramon Grau San Martin

In 1947, Fidel finally decided to join a political group. He joined a group called the Orthodox Party. Its leader was Eduardo Chibas. He was a member of the government. But he wanted Cuba to have honest leaders and create a better life for Cubans, just like Fidel.

Besides wanting to bring change to Cuba, Fidel was also interested in what was happening in other parts of Latin America.

In the spring of 1948, he and several other students traveled to Bogota, Colombia, for a student conference. The conference had been organized to protest the influence of the United States in certain areas of the world.

Latin America

The United States was the most powerful country in the world. It had lots of money and a large army. The United States often asked smaller, less powerful countries for favors, like selling goods to the United States at a low price and allowing US troops to set up army bases. The smaller countries were afraid of what would happen if they said no to the United States.

While Fidel was in Colombia, a beloved leader of Colombia's working classes was shot. Riots broke out after people heard the news.

Fidel and his friends were amazed as they watched the rioters set fires, overturn cars, and attack government buildings. Did Fidel think this was wrong? No. He admired the violent protests.

Fidel and the others saw firsthand the extreme action people took when they were dedicated to a cause and would do anything to support it. Fidel later said, "I was filled with revolutionary fervor."

When Fidel returned to Havana, he campaigned for Eduardo Chibas. Chibas was running for president. The election was to take place on June 1, 1948. Fidel traveled across Cuba with Chibas. He often spoke before Chibas at rallies. Fidel was disappointed when

Eduardo Chibas

Chibas lost the election. However, it did not change his desire to bring change to Cuba.

CHAPTER 3
Rebel with a Cause

Fidel had fallen in love with politics while at the university. And he had also fallen in love. Mirta Diaz-Balart was a philosophy student. (Philosophy is the study of the meaning of life.) She loved Fidel, but she was not interested in politics.

Mirta was from an important and wealthy family. Her father was the mayor of a town not far from the Castro plantation. Mirta's father was not happy about her relationship with an outspoken, rebellious man. He thought Fidel was a troublemaker.

Fidel's father, however, was excited that his son might be connected to an important family. When Fidel and Mirta were married on October 12, 1948, Angel threw a big party for them.

On September 1, 1949, Mirta gave birth to a son. Mirta and Fidel named him Felix Fidel, but they called him Fidelito. (The nickname means "Little Fidel.") Although he was now a husband and a father, Fidel spent very little time with his family. Politics was becoming his life. Instead of finding a job and supporting Mirta and Fidelito, Fidel spent much of his time at the headquarters of the Orthodox Party.

Fidel and Mirta both came from rich families, and they could have asked their parents for money. But Fidel did not want to rely on their wealth. He wanted a simple life for his family. He wanted to be an example to others.

In the fall of 1950, Fidel graduated with a law degree from the University of Havana. It had not been easy for Fidel get through university. He hadn't studied much, skipped classes, and sometimes didn't take exams. But his time there helped to prepare him for the rest of his life.

Fidel soon opened a law office in Havana. He took on cases that would help the poor. Fidel wanted others to see him as a voice for the working class. A hero of the people.

Fidel also decided to run for a seat in the Cuban House of Representatives. He had become an important member of the Orthodox Party. Both

Fidel and the party felt he would win the seat.

The leader of the Orthodox Party at the time was Roberto Agramonte. He was running for president against Fulgencio Batista.

Batista had been the president of the

Fulgencio Batista

country from 1940 to 1944. He had been living in Florida since that time. The polls showed he had little chance of winning the election.

The Cuban people, however, were in for a great shock.

Three months before the election, Batista staged a coup (say: "COO"). (That means he suddenly seized power.) He took control of the government with the help of the Cuban army. Cubans were surprised by Batista's action, but they did not protest. In fact, many Cubans were happy. While president, Batista had built roads, hospitals, and schools in the country.

But as soon as Batista took power, Cubans saw their hopes crushed. Batista threw anyone who opposed him in jail. He got rid of political parties. He controlled the press. And he also took money for government projects and kept it for himself.

Now Fidel had no hope of winning a seat in the House of Representatives. He was furious at what had happened. In Cuba, the chance for a fair government with honest leaders had disappeared. Fidel started to believe that the only way to take power was by force. Bringing change in a peaceful way—through elections—was not going to work. Fidel vowed to overthrow Batista and save Cuba with an armed revolution.

CHAPTER 4
From Follower to Leader

Fidel was very open about his hatred of Batista. He organized marches against Cuba's president. He raised money and gathered weapons to help his own cause.

Soon a thousand people had joined Fidel's movement. They called themselves "Fidelistas." The Fidelistas wanted to overthrow Batista. And who was the most loyal of the Fidelistas? Raul. By this time, he had left college and joined his older brother's growing group of followers.

Fidel was able to win over so many people just by his strong personality. He had a lot of charisma.

When he spoke, Fidel made them believe that anything was possible. Fidel also had movie-star good looks, was more than six feet tall, and had a large build. He gave off a real sense of power.

Fidel's plan was to go to Santiago, a city at the very eastern end of the island. There he would attack the Moncada military barracks while Raul and other Fidelistas would take over government buildings, such as the Palace of Justice. Afterward,

Moncada Barracks

Fidel would announce their victory from the radio station at Moncada. Fidel believed that news of the raid would inspire people all over Cuba to rise up against Batista.

Less than two hundred Fidelistas would take part in the raid. But there were more than seven hundred government soldiers at the barracks. Some of Fidel's followers were worried. How

could their small group win a battle against so many soldiers? But Fidel assured them they would be successful. Once again his powerful personality won over his followers. So on July 24, 1953, Fidel and the small group of Fidelistas traveled from Havana to Santiago. Santiago was almost six hundred miles to the east, and the journey would take several days.

Early on the morning of July 26, Fidel and his band of rebels rode in twenty-six cars toward the Moncada Barracks. They were after the weapons stored there. But most of the drivers were unfamiliar with the city. And at the building where they thought weapons were stored, they discovered a barbershop!

The soldiers guarding the barracks began shooting at them. Many of the rebels, including Fidel, escaped to the nearby Sierra Maestra mountains. However, eight of Fidel's followers were killed, and many more were captured.

Those who were captured were put in prison. Some were put to death.

As for Raul's group, which was to invade the nearby Palace of Justice, they got lost. So did a group that was to storm a hospital and another set of barracks.

Five days after the unsuccessful raid, Batista's soldiers found Fidel. He was arrested and put on trial in Havana.

Fidel's first attempt to stage a revolt ended in total failure.

CHAPTER 5
Prison!

The charge against Fidel was very serious. He had tried to overthrow the government. That was treason.

During the trial, Fidel decided not to use a lawyer in court. He would speak for himself.

Fidel argued with the government lawyers and the judge. He spoke out against Batista. He said he was following in the footsteps of other Cuban heroes, such as Jose Marti. Marti had been a leader in Cuba's fight for independence from Spain.

At the end of his trial, Fidel said, "Condemn me! It does not matter! History will absolve me!" (*Absolve* means to forgive someone.)

On October 16, 1953, Fidel received a fifteen-year prison sentence. He was sent to a prison on an island off the southern coast of Cuba. Raul landed in prison, too.

Fidel decided that if he was to be in prison for so long, his time had to be spent wisely. He read fourteen to fifteen hours a day. He started a school for other prisoners. He gave classes on history and philosophy. Fidel also wrote down his own speeches from his trial. He wanted these speeches to serve as the manifesto for the Cuban Revolution. (A manifesto is public statement

of someone's beliefs.) Fidel had the manifesto
smuggled out of the prison. He wrote the words
in lemon juice, and they were revealed by putting
a hot iron on the paper. His supporters made
copies and handed them out all over Cuba.

Fidel's plans for his country were read all across Cuba. Fidel was becoming famous. His name was known to citizens everywhere.

While in prison, Fidel learned that Mirta had been working for the Batista government. Fidel was shocked that his wife would do something that was against his beliefs. He felt betrayed, and then and there, he decided to divorce Mirta.

A Very Private Life

Part of Fidel's life was very public. He stood in front of thousands of people giving speeches, and he made many appearances on TV. But Fidel kept his personal life very private. He was always afraid that his enemies wanted to kill him. Because of this, Fidel had many houses around the country, and he never stayed in the same house for more than one night.

Fidel and his first wife, Mirta, divorced in 1955. After that, Fidel was involved with several women throughout his life. His relationship with Dalia Soto del Valle lasted more than forty years. It is

Dalia Soto del Valle

unknown if they were married, but they did have five children together. Fidel also had children with other women he did not marry.

Also, it looked like Fidel lived a simple life like every other Cuban. But it is rumored that he actually was a very wealthy man and was worth millions of dollars when he died.

In November 1954, Batista held elections in Cuba. No one was allowed to run against him, so of course Batista won. He felt confident about his power and control over Cuba. Because of this, he made a surprising decision. Batista released political prisoners, including Fidel, Raul, and the Fidelistas. This decision changed the future of Cuba forever.

CHAPTER 6
Freedom!

On May 15, 1955, after less than two years in prison, Fidel was free. He went back to Havana. He was hailed as a hero because he had stood up to Batista.

Fidel continued to speak out against Batista and the Cuban government. And now Fidel gave his revolution a name. He called it the 26th of July Movement.

This was in honor of the Fidelistas who had died during the raid at the Moncada Barracks.

Many of Fidel's speeches were printed in newspapers. Now Batista clearly understood that freeing Fidel had been a terrible decision. So he threatened to put Fidel, Raul, and their followers back in jail. He also said newspapers that printed Fidel's speeches would be shut down.

Fidel saw that he was putting his life and the lives of his followers at risk. Raul was accused of blowing up a movie theater in Havana. The charge was false. Batista's agents had planted the bomb. To avoid arrest, Raul fled to Mexico City. Fidel decided that he would also be safer in Mexico. So he joined Raul and some other followers who were already there.

While in Mexico, Fidel stayed in touch with his supporters in Cuba. A new plan was needed to get rid of Batista once and for all. Fidel and his followers had to be better organized than they

had been at the Moncada Barracks. So Fidel and
the rebels studied the ways of guerrilla warfare.
They would need to take Batista and the Cuban
army by complete surprise.

Training a rebel army would cost money. In
October 1955, Fidel visited the United States
to raise money for the cause. Many Cubans had
fled to the United States to escape Batista and his
policies. They were happy to help Fidel with his
revolution.

Guerrilla Warfare

In Spanish, the word *guerrilla* means "little war." Guerrilla warfare is a type of fighting often used by small groups that don't have a lot of weapons or money. These small groups rely on surprise attacks to defeat large troops of trained soldiers. The guerrillas avoid traditional styles of fighting where troops face one another across a battlefield. Guerrillas change their location and direction of attack to confuse their enemy. Guerrilla forces often strike their enemy from hiding places like mountains or caves. Many of Fidel's

guerrilla soldiers came from the poor villages and towns around the Sierra Maestra mountains.

Fidel's plans for revolution were coming together. He and his followers were ready to go back to Cuba.

The time for action was now!

Che Guevara

During his time in Mexico, Fidel met Ernesto "Che" Guevara, a young doctor who was from Argentina. Che  had heard about Fidel. He was impressed by Fidel and his idea of overthrowing the government of Batista. Che and Fidel quickly became close friends. They often sat up all night talking about politics. Che decided to join Fidel's group of revolutionaries.

Che was a thinker and a planner. Fidel was a born leader and a great speaker. They worked well together. Che helped Fidel with his plans to overthrow Batista. Later Che became involved in guerrilla warfare in Bolivia. He was arrested and put to death in 1967.

CHAPTER 7
Viva Fidel

With some of the money that Fidel had raised, he bought a boat called the *Granma*. It was meant to carry only twelve passengers. But on the night of November 25, 1956, Fidel, Raul, and eighty revolutionaries got on board. They started out from Tuxpan Harbor in Mexico and headed for Cuba.

Fidel had alerted his followers in Cuba that he would arrive on November 30. But on the journey, a storm struck. The boat struggled in the rough seas. Fidel was going to arrive in Cuba much later than planned. So what did Fidel's followers in Cuba do? They started the revolution—without their leader!

The *Granma* finally made it to Cuba on December 2. Not only was Fidel late, the boat was more than a mile away from the beach where it was supposed to land. Then the boat ran aground on a mud bank. Fidel and his revolutionaries had to jump off and make their way to shore. Fidel later recalled, "This wasn't a landing, it was a shipwreck!"

And who was waiting for Fidel and his men? Batista's forces!

Batista had learned of the rebels' plan and was ready for them. Airplanes and patrol boats shot at Fidel and his men. The revolutionaries fled into the nearby mountains. They found a hideout, but on December 5, the government army caught up with them. Many were killed or captured. Some ran away for good. Once again, Fidel's plans had failed.

Only Fidel, Raul, and fewer than twenty other men escaped. This small group retreated farther into the mountains. There they met many men and women who had hard lives. They were eager to join Fidel's cause. They believed Fidel's promise that his revolution would give them better lives.

Even while hiding in the mountains, Fidel made sure that the world knew about his work. He invited reporters to come and visit him. In February 1957, Herbert Matthews of the *New York Times* interviewed Fidel.

Cuban Rebel Is Visited in Hideout

Fidel pretended to have many more followers than he did. He also told some of his troops to interrupt the interview and give him important-sounding messages. In his article, Herbert Matthews said, "President Fulgencio Batista . . .

is fighting a losing battle to destroy the most dangerous enemy he has yet faced."

The next showdown came in May of 1958. Batista sent ten thousand men into the Sierra Maestra mountains to stop Castro for good.

At first Batista's troops were beating Fidel's small band. But that changed. As the battles moved deeper into the mountains, Fidel's troops started winning. They knew the mountain terrain

and were able to surprise the government troops, using the methods of guerrilla warfare. Many people who lived in the mountains also let Fidel and his troops know where the government troops were.

By the end of July, Fidel decided it was time to spread his forces across the country. Some headed west; some headed to the center of the island; and Fidel, with Raul's help, led other troops to the east.

As 1958 drew to a close, it became clear that the government army couldn't stop Fidel and his rebels. Batista was afraid of what would happen to him if Fidel's forces captured him.

So on New Year's Eve, Batista threw one last party. He chose this moment to tell his guests the big news. He was going to resign at midnight! He said that anyone who wanted to escape with him had to be at the airport by 2:00 a.m. Early the next morning, on January 1, 1959, Batista and his family got on a plane. They headed to the Dominican Republic. Batista later moved to Portugal and then to Spain. He died there in 1973.

It was over. Fidel and his forces had won!

In the city of Santiago, Fidel was cheered like a hero. With Raul by his side, he slowly made his way west to Havana in an open-top jeep. He stopped along the way to give speeches, always greeted by adoring crowds.

Fidel finally reached Havana on January 9. The streets were filled with people waiting to see their new leader. As he drove past, cheers of *"¡Viva Fidel!"* (Long live Fidel!) and *"¡Viva la revolución!"* (Long live the revolution!) rang out.

A new day had come for Cuba. Or so the people hoped.

CHAPTER 8
From Plans to Action

Did Fidel become the new president of Cuba? No. He did not want to be. But he still was going to be in charge. Fidel chose to become the commander in chief of Cuba's armed forces. He named Manuel Urrutia as president, but he was not nearly as powerful as Fidel. Urrutia was a judge who had often disagreed with Batista.

Urrutia went to work to put a new government and a cabinet in place. Meanwhile, Fidel focused on punishing Batista's supporters. He put Raul and Che Guevara in charge of that.

Raul

Fidel wanted to get rid of any enemies who might challenge him. This was just what Batista had done. Fidel also made speeches on the radio, appeared on TV, and gave interviews to newspapers. He wanted to remind Cuba, and the rest of the world, that *he* had won the revolution. He was Cuba's new leader.

But Fidel had to be careful when it came to Cuba's nearby neighbor, the United States. The US government was worried about a revolutionary in control of a country only ninety miles away. The United States was worried that Fidel wanted to turn Cuba into a communist country.

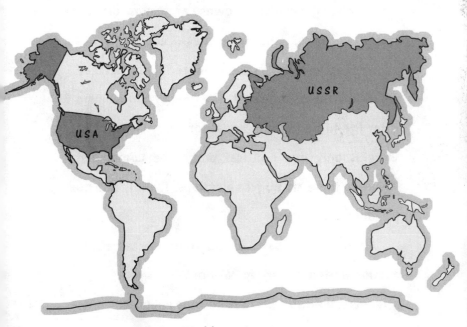

World map in 1960

Communism

In 1922, Russia and
fourteen other countries
joined together to form
a communist state called
the Union of Soviet Socialist

Republics (USSR). Communism is a political system where the government owns and controls all factories, farms, and businesses. People are not allowed to own property. Everyone receives what they need from the government. The goal of communism is for life to be fair and equal for every citizen. But there is only one political party—the Communist Party—so there are no free elections. There is also no freedom of speech.

Although the USSR had fought on the same side as the United States in World War II (1939–45), afterward the two countries became enemies.

People in communist USSR
lining up for food

The United States was very fearful of communism spreading to other countries and the USSR becoming more powerful than America. The US government was determined to stop that from happening.

Fidel visited the United States in April 1959. He wanted to convince the US government and US citizens that Cuba was their friend. In New York City, he gave speeches, saying that he was not a communist. He promised that his new government would not interfere with US companies in Cuba. He also promised that Cuba would support the United States against the

Fidel meets with Vice President Richard Nixon

USSR and communism. The US government was relieved when they heard these words from Fidel.

Did Fidel honor his promises?

No!

On his return to Cuba, he did exactly the opposite. He began turning Cuba into a communist nation. Property was taken away from wealthy landowners and given to the working classes. The Cuban government took over some big businesses, such as the telephone company. And even though Fidel had reassured the US government that Cuba would leave US companies alone, the Cuban government took those over as well.

Newspapers are important because they give readers information. But Fidel became worried about people speaking out against him and his government. So he made changes. Newspapers could criticize his policies. But they also had to print the official position of the new government.

The newspapers were very angry. Fidel was controlling what they could report. But if they didn't go along with what Fidel wanted, he would shut them down.

The working classes were pleased with the changes that Fidel was making. He had given many people land that they could farm. He had also expanded the public school system and made health care available to more people. Life was improving for many of Cuba's poorest citizens.

However, many people in the middle and upper classes were not happy at all. Fidel had taken away what was theirs. Now he also declared that there would not be free elections for four years. More and more, it sounded like Cuba's new leader was turning the country away from democracy and toward communism. Many of these Cubans decided to leave their country and headed to Miami, Florida. There they created their own "Little Havana," which became a home away from home.

The United States was happy to accept these Cuban refugees because a lot of Fidel's changes were hurting as many citizens as they helped. The United States, which had supported Cuba until now, became unfriendly toward Cuba.

Fidel was angry about losing the support of the United States. But he soon realized that he could rely on another country to help with his plans for Cuba: the country that was the United States' biggest enemy—the USSR.

CHAPTER 9
Friends and Enemies

Shortly after Fidel came to power, he offered to sell some of Cuba's sugar crop to the USSR. Soon Cuba was selling more than one million tons of sugar to the USSR each year. In exchange, Cuba received goods such as fuel oil, paper, steel, aluminum, and wheat. These were all things that Cuba needed but did not produce itself.

Anastas Mikoyan of the USSR with Fidel

Nikita Khrushchev

In September 1960, Fidel was invited to represent Cuba at a meeting at the United Nations in New York City. One of the reasons he accepted was because Nikita Khrushchev, the leader of the USSR, would be there. It would give the two men a chance to talk face-to-face.

Fidel and Khrushchev were photographed hugging each other and laughing. Officials in the US government were angry. This was a sign from Fidel that Cuba did not need the United States. Cuba could now rely on the world's other superpower.

The United States wanted to get back at Fidel

for his closeness with the USSR. So except for sending some medicine and food, the United States stopped all trade with Cuba. Fidel declared to the citizens of Cuba that this was a sign that

The Miami Herald

**Cuban Blockade Ordered;
JFK Warns of War Peril**

JFK's 7-Point
Program on Cuba

*Food, Medicine
Only Commodities
Allowed to Pass*

the United States was going to attack Cuba. He said the military needed to be ready.

Although the United States was not preparing to invade Cuba, they did have a plot to get rid of Fidel. Rather than using US military troops, the United States was going to have Cuban exiles (people who had fled Cuba) lead the raid. This way the US government could claim to not be involved. The USSR could not blame the United States for trying to overthrow their new friend.

The exiles were given money and guns, and trained at a US army camp. All of this was very secret. It was so secret that the new US president, John F. Kennedy, only learned about it after he took office in January of 1961. President Kennedy had spoken out against Cuba during his campaign. Although he had doubts about the plan, he felt he had to go ahead with it.

John F. Kennedy

He had to stand up to Cuba.

On April 17, 1,511 Cuban exiles that the United States had trained landed on two beaches in Cuba. The area was called the Bay of Pigs.

But Fidel learned of the Central Intelligence Agency's (CIA's) scheme. His troops were ready for the invasion. They attacked the exiles from the air and on land. The exiles had no chance of winning unless the US government came to their rescue. But President Kennedy did not want to send US troops to Cuba.

Most of the Cuban exiles were captured. They revealed the attacks had been planned by the US government. The victory of Fidel's troops over the United States made him even more popular with the Cuban people.

The CIA

Founded in 1947, the Central Intelligence Agency, or CIA, is part of the US government. The people who work for the CIA gather and analyze information from around the world. This information, or intelligence, helps US leaders make decisions about their relationships with other countries. Much of the work the CIA does is secret. The people who do this work are spies. The CIA also works to stop spies from other countries gathering secret information about the US. Today, the CIA focuses a lot on preventing terrorism and cyber terrorism (computer hacking).

The fact that the United States had organized this plot made Fidel distrust the United States even more. He now thought that the United States would do anything to get rid of him. To anger the United States, Fidel decided he would work more closely with the USSR.

In the summer of 1962, Cuba made an agreement with the USSR: The USSR could build nuclear missile bases in Cuba and send over missiles. These missiles would be able to reach the United States in minutes. They were powerful enough to destroy entire cities.

A couple of months later, US spy planes were taking photos of Cuba. The photographs revealed that there were Russian missile bases just ninety miles away from the United States.

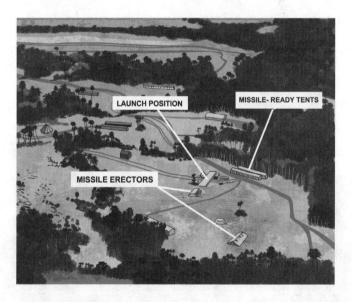

President Kennedy demanded that the USSR remove the missiles. He warned that if the USSR attacked the United States, the United States would strike back at the USSR. To show he meant business, President Kennedy ordered US navy ships to surround the island of Cuba. They would stop any Russian ship carrying missiles that came within five hundred miles of Cuba.

Khrushchev had already sent more ships. He did not want to back down, but he also did not want to start a nuclear war. The world held its breath during the standoff. At the last minute,

Khrushchev told the Russian ships to turn around. The world's two superpowers had avoided a war. The Cuban Missile Crisis was over.

When Fidel heard the news, he kicked a wall so hard, he broke a mirror. Why was he so angry? The missile problem had been settled without him. Fidel felt Cuba had been used by the United States and the USSR. Like a pawn in a chess game.

CHAPTER 10
Hard Times

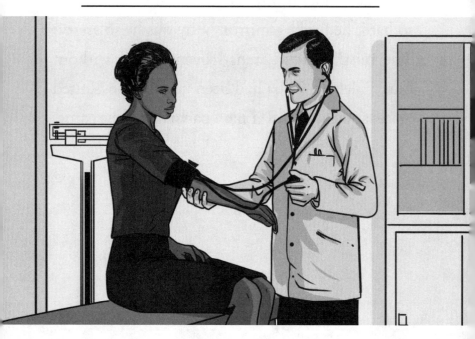

Although some of Fidel's plans for Cuba were successful, others failed. Free education and health care became available to more Cubans. But Cuba's economy was a mess. The country was unable to grow the food it needed to feed its citizens. Most farmland was used to grow sugar cane. And Cuba did not manufacture the goods that businesses needed, such as trucks and building materials.

In 1969, Fidel came up with a new plan that he was sure would succeed. It was called the "Ten-Million-Ton Harvest." Now each year the country would work to harvest ten million tons of sugar cane. That was way more than in any previous year. But over the next seven years, the sugar cane harvest in Cuba fell. The Ten-Million-Ton Harvest plan was a bust.

Fidel took total responsibility for the failure. He told the Cuban people that maybe it was time for him to resign. But despite the country's struggles, Fidel was still their hero. And because the people loved him, he knew he could do pretty much anything he wanted.

So in the mid-1970s, Fidel decided to change the way Cuba's government worked. He did this by rewriting the constitution. (A constitution lays out the laws and rules of a country's government.) The new constitution made it look like Fidel was giving Cuban citizens and the government more freedom, like open elections. But really it did the exact opposite. The only people who could run for office had to agree with the policies of Fidel and his party—the Communist Party of Cuba. And no one wanted to take the risk of running against Fidel, who was now in charge of the entire government. So he had pretty much made himself the official president and leader of Cuba for life.

He held the power. No one else.

In 1979, Fidel traveled to New York City to speak at the United Nations again. He knew this was an opportunity to remind the world of his power. He spoke for two hours. He said the rich countries of the world had to end hunger, poverty, corruption, and disease in the poorer countries.

The truth was, people in Cuba were suffering from these very problems. The freedoms and better life that Fidel had promised never came true.

On April 1, 1980, six people who were tired of Fidel's empty promises took action. They crashed

a bus into the gates at the Embassy of Peru in Havana. They asked the embassy to protect them from Fidel and his harsh policies. Over the next three days, more than ten thousand Cubans who wanted to leave their homeland showed up at the embassy.

The Peruvian Embassy in Havana

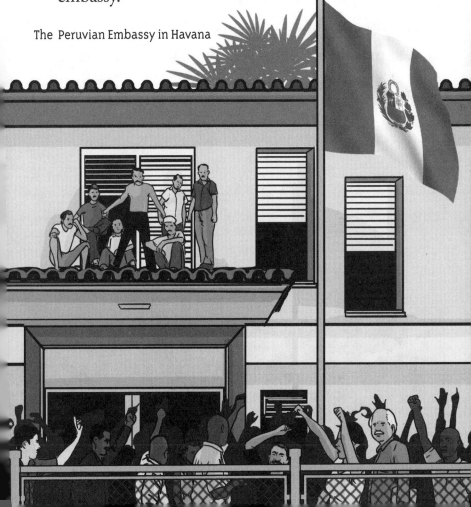

Fidel was worried that more citizens might decide to stand up to him. So on April 21, he declared that any citizen who wanted to leave Cuba was free to do so. He was saying, "If you want to go, then go." He didn't believe many would. However, Fidel—and the world—was surprised by how many people fled the country. US president Jimmy Carter agreed to accept 3,500 refugees. And over the next few months,

more than 120,000 people crowded onto boats to find a better life. This made Fidel furious.

In November 1980, Ronald Reagan was elected president of the United States. He was fiercely anti-Communist. He learned that Cuba and the USSR were building an airport on Grenada, an island off the coast of South America.

To Reagan, this meant that Cuba and the USSR were trying to spread communism to new places.

Reagan wouldn't stand for that. So US troops were sent to Grenada on October 26, 1983. The US soldiers captured more than six hundred Cubans and sent them home.

But the biggest blow for Fidel came when
Mikhail Gorbachev, who was then the leader
of the USSR, announced that his country's
government needed to change. He called for

glasnost (openness) and *perestroika* (remaking the political system). Fidel realized that with the USSR following this path, Cuba would be left alone without the support of its greatest friend. Cuba would no longer receive needed goods from the USSR, and it would have no one to buy most of its sugar. Cuba was facing a disaster.

CHAPTER 11
Fidel Steps Down

In December 1991, the USSR broke apart. What had once been one huge communist nation became fifteen separate countries. The result was that Cuba lost almost $6 billion in aid. The country could no longer rely on the USSR sending them oil.

This sent Cuba's economy plunging. Poor people became even poorer. Goods were rationed (allowing each person to have only a fixed amount of something), so people could not always get the things they needed, such as food, fuel, and clothing. Fidel knew he had to do something. Especially since the US government was waiting for Fidel's government to collapse.

Fidel decided to help increase tourism in Cuba. Tourists who visited the island would spend money in the country. This way the country could help reduce its debts. But the growth in tourism brought more troubles to Cuba. Many educated

Cubans, such as lawyers and engineers, realized they could make more money as taxi drivers or waiters. Jobs that helped the tourist industry paid more money than their regular jobs. There were now lots of people to wait on tables and drive taxis, but there weren't enough people to try cases in court or design roads and buildings.

Cuba had hit really hard times. So some world leaders, including former US president Jimmy Carter and Pope John Paul II, began to speak out against the United States' ban on trade with Cuba. They felt that this policy hurt

Pope John Paul II

the Cuban people more than it hurt Fidel. Maybe it was time for the United States and Cuba to try to improve their relationship.

Elian Gonzalez

On November 25, 1999, Elian Gonzalez was found
floating in an inner
tube off the coast
of Florida. Elian, his
mother, and eleven
other people were
trying to escape Cuba
to find a better life
in the United States.
During the journey,
the raft they were on

flipped over. Elian, who was five years old, was the
only person to survive.

Elian's parents were divorced. Elian's father, who
lived in Cuba, wanted his son sent back there. But
Elian's relatives in Miami—relatives on his mother's
side—wanted him to stay in the United States. Both

the US and Cuban governments got involved in the fight. Citizens in both countries held protests. The battle over Elian lasted months. Finally, the US Supreme Court got involved. It declared that Elian should return to Cuba and live with his father. On June 28, 2000, Elian went back to Havana.

The United States did soften. The trade ban was still kept in place, but starting in 2000, US companies were allowed to sell food to Cuba, food that the country didn't grow itself. This helped make life less difficult for many Cuban citizens.

By this time, Fidel was in his seventies, and people started to wonder about his health. In June 2001, he fainted in front of thousands of people in Havana. He broke his arm and knee three years later when he fell off a stage after giving a speech. In 2006, after having surgery, Fidel turned power over to his brother Raul. He said that this was only temporary. He would go back to running the country as soon as he was better. But on February 19, 2008, at the age of eighty-one, Fidel officially resigned. He was one of the world's longest-ruling leaders.

CHAPTER 12
Hero or Villain?

Fidel was hardly ever seen after Raul took over. There were often rumors that Fidel had died. Whenever those rumors popped up, Fidel made sure that photographs of him appeared in the newspapers or on websites. In April 2016, he attended the Communist Party of Cuba meeting in Havana. It was clear that Fidel was very frail and sick.

Fidel died seven months later on November
25, 2016. He was ninety years old, and yet his
death was still a shock. Especially for the people

of Cuba. For so many Cuban citizens, he was the only leader they had ever known. For many, Fidel *was* Cuba.

After his death, a lot was written about the kind of person Fidel was and what he had done for Cuba. Yes, he had been a brave young leader. But he turned into a ruthless dictator, a ruler in total control. Fidel sent thousands of political opponents to prison. He did not allow free elections or freedom of speech. Fidel did give the Cuban people better schools and more access to medical care. Yet in so many other ways, he didn't really improve the lives of poor Cubans as he'd promised.

So was Fidel a hero or a villain? The answer is: It depends on who you ask. And whether you think he was a hero or a villain, his influence on Cuba, Latin America, and the world was huge. Fidel's name will live on in history.

Timeline of Fidel Castro's Life

1926	Fidel Castro is born near Biran, Cuba, on August 13
1933	Attends La Salle boarding school in Santiago, Cuba
1940	Attends Dolores Academy, Santiago, Cuba
1942	Attends Jesuit preparatory school of Belen in Havana, Cuba
1945	Enters the University of Havana to study law
1950	Graduates from university and opens a law office
1953	Leads an unsuccessful coup and is sentenced to fifteen years in prison
1956	Sails from Mexico to Cuba with a group of revolutionaries
1959	Overthrows the Cuban government, and President Fulgencio Batista flees Cuba
1961	Bay of Pigs invasion by US troops fails to overthrow Fidel Castro
1962	The USSR threatens to place nuclear missiles in Cuba, starting the Cuban Missile Crisis
1980	125,000 Cuban refugees leave the country
2000	Fights for return of Elian Gonzalez to his father in Cuba
2005	Gives a five-hour speech where he denies being ill
2006	Transfers power to his brother Raul
2008	Resigns as president of Cuba, and Raul is named president
2016	Dies in Havana on November 25

Timeline of the World

1929	The US stock market crashes, setting off the Great Depression
1936	Spanish Civil War begins
1939	World War II begins, Spanish Civil War ends
1945	World War II ends
1949	The formation of the People's Republic of China
1953	Joseph Stalin, leader of the USSR, dies
1963	US president John F. Kennedy is assassinated
1981	First woman, Sandra Day O'Connor, appointed to the US Supreme Court
1991	Collapse of the USSR
1994	The end of apartheid in South Africa
2001	World Trade Center and Pentagon attacks
2008	Barack Obama is elected the first African American president of the United States
2010	Major earthquake in Haiti kills hundreds of thousands
2016	Obama says trade embargo with Cuba should be lifted
	Donald Trump elected president of the United States

Bibliography

* Books for young readers

*Blue, Rose, and Corinne J. Naden. *Fidel Castro and the Cuban Revolution*. Greensboro, NC: Morgan Reynolds Publishing, 2006.

Castro, Fidel, and Ignacio Ramonet. *Fidel Castro: My Life*. New York: Scribner, 2008.

Coltman, Leycester. *The Real Fidel Castro*. London: Thistle Publishing, 2013.

DePalma, Anthony. "Fidel Castro, Cuban Revolutionary Who Defied U.S., Dies at 90." *New York Times*, November 26, 2016. http://www.nytimes.com/2016/11/26/world/americas/fidel-castro-dies.html.

"Fidel Castro." *Encyclopaedia Britannica Online*. Last modified April 11, 2017. http://www.britannica.com/biography/Fidel-Castro.

"Fidel Castro Biography.com." *Biography.com*. Last modified December 5, 2016. http://www.biography.com/people/fidel-castro-9241487.

"Fidel Castro, Cuba's Leader of Revolution, Dies at 90." *BBC News*, November 26, 2016. http://www.bbc.com/news/world-latin-america-38114953.

*Marsico, Katie. *Fidel Castro: Cuban President & Revolutionary*. Minneapolis: ABDO Publishing, 2009.

*Platt, Richard. *Fidel Castro: From Guerrilla to World Statesman*. Austin, TX: Raintree Steck-Vaughn Publishers, 2003.

*Rees, Fran. *Fidel Castro: Leader of Communist Cuba*. Minneapolis: Compass Point Books, 2006.